contemporary *vocal* groups

ISBN 0-634-01713-6

HAL•LEONARD®
CORPORATION
7777 W. BLUEMOUND RD. P.O. BOX 13819 MILWAUKEE, WI 53213

Visit Hal Leonard Online at
www.halleonard.com

contemporary *vocal* groups

contents

BILLS, BILLS, BILLS

Words and Music by KANDI L. BURRUSS,
KEVIN BRIGGS, BEYONCE KNOWLES,
KELLY ROWLAND and LeTOYA LUCKETT

Moderately, half-time feel

At first we start-ed out real cool,
Now you've been max-in' out my card,

tak-in' me plac-es I had nev-er___ been.___ But now___
gave me bad cred-it, buy me gifts with__ my___ own name.__

BRING IT ALL TO ME

Words and Music by KEVIN SPENCER,
WILLIAM SHELBY, NIDRA BEARD, LINDA CARRIERE,
CORY ROONEY, B. LAWRENCE, V. RUBY and L. LEWIS

* Male vocal written one octave lower than sung throughout.

I'll put my pride to the side just to

tell you how good you make me feel in - side.

(Male:) There's not a sin - gle ques - tion that we

can't make this right 'cause it's you I need

BUG A BOO

Words and Music by KANDI L. BURRUSS,
KEVIN BRIGGS, BEYONCE KNOWLES, KELLY ROWLAND,
LE TOYA LUCKETT and LATAVIA ROBERSON

Steadily, half-time feel

(Spoken:) Thou shall not bug.

You make me wan-na throw my pag-er out _ the win-dow, tell _ M - C - I to cut _ the phone poles, break _

Original key: Ab minor. This edition has been transposed up one half-step to be more playable.

CODA

cool. When you call me on the phone, you're bug -

- gin' me. When you fol - low me a - round, you're bug - gin' me.

Ev - 'ry - thing you do be bug - gin' me. You're bug - gin' me. You're bug -

- gin' me. When you show up at my door, you're bug - gin' me. When you

C'EST LA VIE

Words and Music by RAY HEDGES,
MARTIN BRANNIGAN, TRACY ACKERMAN and B*WITCHED

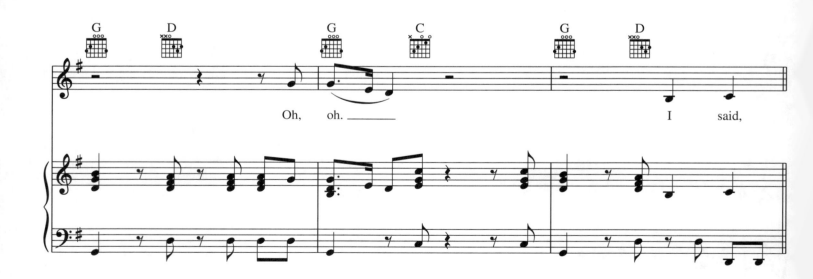

CLEOPATRA'S THEME

Words and Music by CLEOPATRA LYNVEST, ZAINAM HIGGINS,
YONAH LYNVEST, TIM SCRAFTON and KENNY HAYES

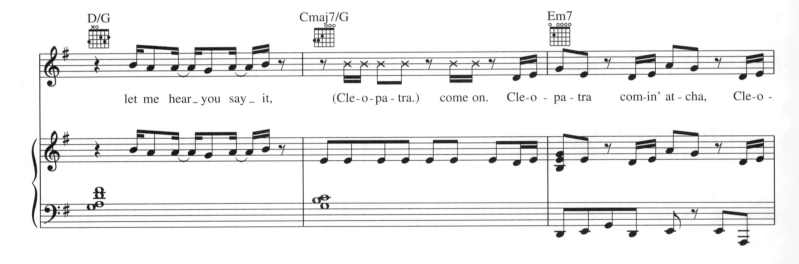

Original key: E♭ minor. This edition has been transposed up one half-step to be more playable.

CREEP

Words and Music by
DALLAS AUSTIN

Moderately

Oh, __ oh, __ oh, __ yeah. Oh, __ oh, __ oh, __

__ yeah. __ The twen-ty-sec-ond of lone - li - ness and we've been __
creep. The twen-ty-third of lone - li - ness and we don't talk

__ through so __ man - y things. I love my man with all hon -
__ like we __ used to do. Now this is pret - ty strange,

THE HARDEST THING

Words and Music by STEVE KIPNER
and DAVID FRANK

DIGGIN' ON YOU

Words and Music by
BABYFACE

END OF THE ROAD
from the Paramount Motion Picture BOOMERANG

Words and Music by BABYFACE,
L.A. REID and DARYL SIMMONS

(Spoken:) Girl, you know we belong together.

I don't have no time for you to be playin' with my heart like this.   You'll be mine forever, baby, you just see.

1. We be-long to-geth-er   and you know   that I'm right.
2. Girl, I know you real-ly love me,   you just don't   re-al-ize.
3. *See additional lyrics*

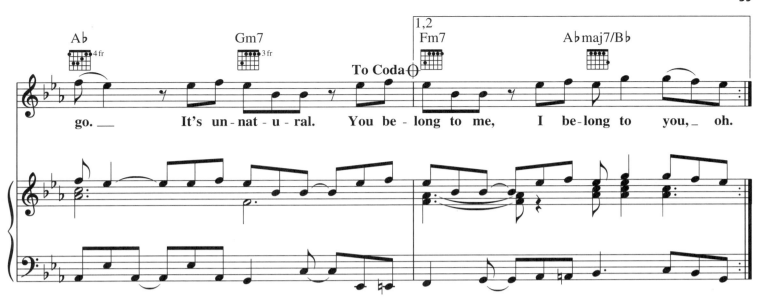

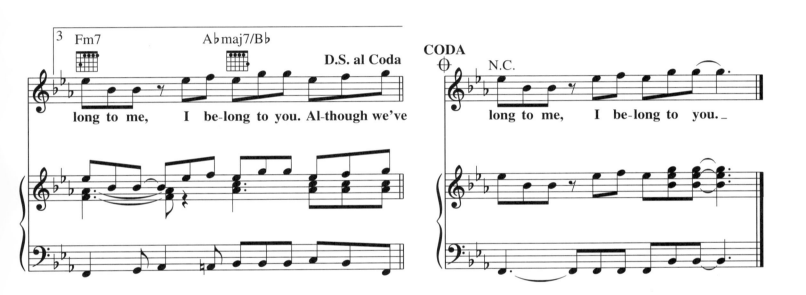

Additional Lyrics

(Spoken:) Girl, I'm here for you.
    All those times at night when you just hurt me,
    And just ran out with that other fellow,
    Baby, I knew about it.
    I just didn't care.
    You just don't understand how much I love you, do you?
    I'm here for you.
    I'm not out to go out there and cheat all night just like you did, baby.
    But that's alright, huh, I love you anyway.
    And I'm still gonna be here for you 'til my dyin' day, baby.
    Right now, I'm just in so much pain, baby.
    'Cause you just won't come back to me, will you?
    Just come back to me.

    Yes, baby, my heart is lonely.
    My heart hurts, baby, yes, I feel pain too.
    Baby please...

4 SEASONS OF LONELINESS

Words and Music by JAMES HARRIS III
and TERRY LEWIS

Lyrics: I long __ for the warmth __ of days __ gone by __

Original key: D♭ major. This edition has been transposed up one half-step to be more playable.

watch   four   sea - sons (1.,2.) change. _____
                          (3.) gain. _____
              (1.-3.)   In comes the win - ter breeze that   chills the air   and drifts the snow.

And I i - mag - ine kiss - ing   you un - der the mis - tle - toe.   When spring-time makes its way here

li - lac blooms re - mind me of the   scent   of your ___ per - fume. _____

When sum - mer burns with heat I   al - ways get the hots for you.   Go skin - ny - dip - pin' in the

HAVE A LITTLE MERCY

Words and Music by JAMES HARRIS III
and TERRY LEWIS

I DRIVE MYSELF CRAZY

Words and Music by RICK NOWELS,
ELLEN SHIPLEY and ALAN RICH

I WANT YOU BACK

Words and Music by DENNIS POP
and MAX MARTIN

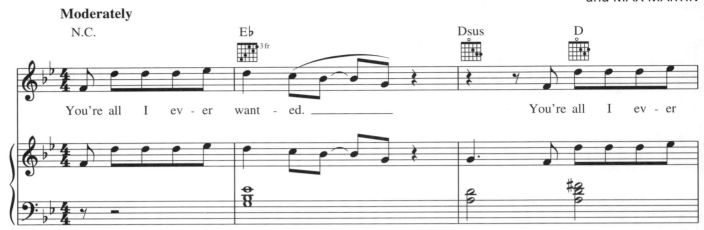

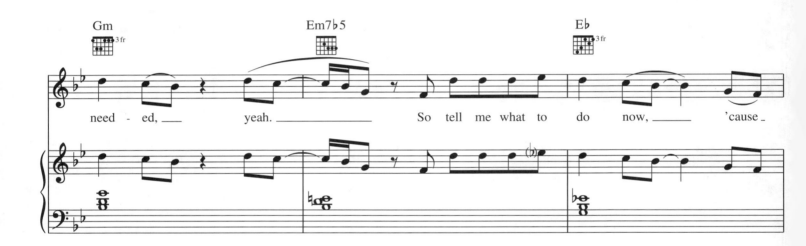

Original key: G♯ minor. This edition has been transposed down one half-step to be more playable.

I'LL MAKE LOVE TO YOU

Words and Music by
BABYFACE

Slowly, in a steady 2

Close your eyes, make a wish, and blow
lax, let's go slow. I ain't

IF YOU LOVE ME

Words and Music by KEIRSTON JAMAL LEWIS
and STOKLEY MANDELLA WILLIAMS

Original key: G# major. This edition has been transposed down one half-step to be more playable.

I'M STILL IN LOVE WITH YOU

Words and Music by JAMES HARRIS III
and TERRY LEWIS

IN THE STILL OF THE NITE
(I'LL REMEMBER)

Words and Music by
FRED PARRIS

INVISIBLE MAN

Words and Music by SEAN HOSEIN,
DANE DeVILLER and STEPHEN KIPNER

in - to mine, _____ tell - ing me more than an - y

words could say. _____ But you don't e - ven know I'm a - live. _____

Ba - by, to you all I am is the in - vis - i - ble man. _

You don't see_ me, ba -

NO MATTER WHAT

from WHISTLE DOWN THE WIND

Music by ANDREW LLOYD WEBBER
Lyrics by JIM STEINMAN

No mat-ter what they tell us, no mat-ter what they do,
If on-ly tears were laugh-ter, if on-ly night was day,

no mat-ter what they teach us, what we be-lieve is true.
if on-ly prayers were an-swered then we would hear God say.

I know our love's for-ev-er,
No mat-ter where it's bar-ren

I know no mat-ter what.
our dream is be-ing born.

NO SCRUBS

Words and Music by KANDI L. BURRUSS,
TAMEKA COTTLE and KEVIN BRIGGS

Original key: G♯ minor. This edition has been transposed down one half-step to be more playable.

ONE SWEET DAY

Words and Music by MARIAH CAREY,
WALTER AFANASIEFF, SHAWN STOCKMAN,
MICHAEL McCARY, NATHAN MORRIS and WANYA MORRIS

Al - though the sun will nev - er shine _ the same, _

I'll al - ways look to a bright - er day. _____ Lord, I ___ know _ when I

lay me down _ to sleep, _____ you will al - ways lis - ten _____ as I

pray. ___ And I know you're shin - ing down on me from

READY TO RUN
from the Paramount Motion Picture RUNAWAY BRIDE

Words and Music by MARTIE SEIDEL
and MARCUS HUMMON

read - y _____ this time. _____

(read - y this time _____) You see, it

feels like I'm start - in' a - gain. _____ And I'm gon - na be

read - y this time. _____

(read - y this time _____)

Read y, - read y, read - y, read - y read - y to run. _____

oh, _____ I'm read - y to run, _____ I'm read - y.

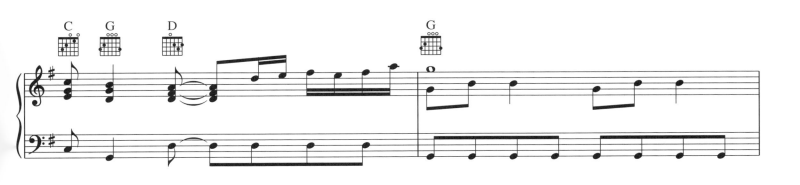

Repeat and Fade

Optional Ending

RED LIGHT SPECIAL

Words and Music by
BABYFACE

SAY MY NAME

Words and Music by RODNEY JERKINS,
LaSHAWN DANIELS, FRED JERKINS,
BEYONCE KNOWLES, LeTOYA LUCKETT,
LATAVIA ROBERSON and KELENDRIA ROWLAND

SAY YOU'LL BE THERE

Words and Music by ELLIOT KENNEDY
and SPICE GIRLS

Am7

D9 4fr

(1.) Last time that we had ___ this con - ver - sa - tion,
(2.) And now you tell me that you're fall - ing in ___ love. Well, I
(D.S.) If you put two and two ___ to - geth - er, you will

Fmaj7

C

I de - cid - ed we should be friends, _____ hey,
nev - er ev - er thought that would be, _____ hey.
see what ___ our friend - ship is for, _____ oh.

Am7

D9 4fr

but now, we're go - ing 'round ___ in cir - cles. Tell me,
This time you got - ta take ___ it eas - y, throw - ing
If you can work this ___ e - qua - tion, then I'll

THE SIGN

Words and Music by buddha,
joker, jenny and linn

Reggae pop

(I,) I got a new _ life. You'd hard-ly rec-og-nize_ me. I'm_ so glad.
(I,) un-der the pale _ moon for so man-y years I won-dered who_ you are.

SOMEDAY
(Pop Version)
from Walt Disney's THE HUNCHBACK OF NOTRE DAME
as recorded by All-4-One

Music by ALAN MENKEN
Lyrics by STEPHEN SCHWARTZ

TEARIN' UP MY HEART

Words and Music by MAX MARTIN
and KRISTIAN LUNDIN

UNPRETTY

Words and Music by DALLAS AUSTIN
and TIONNE WATKINS

I wish I could tie you up __ in my __ shoes, __ make you feel un - pret - ty, too.

Nev - er in - se - cure un - til __ I met __ you. __ Now I'm be - in' stu - pid.

*Vocal line is written an octave higher than sung.

* *Vocal line is written as sung.*

I make you feel un - pret - ty. _____

Oh. _____   Oh,   oh. _____

Oh. _____   Oh,   oh. _____   Oh. _____   Oh,   oh. _____

TOO MUCH

Words and Music by ANDY WATKINS,
PAUL WILSON and SPICE GIRLS

TRUE TO YOUR HEART
(Pop Version)
from Walt Disney Pictures' MULAN
as recorded by 98° featuring Stevie Wonder

Music by MATTHEW WILDER
Lyrics by DAVID ZIPPEL

Ba- by, I knew at once _ that you were meant for me. _ Deep

to your heart.) __

When things are get - tin' cra - zy
When all the world a - round you,

and you don't know where to start, __ keep on be - liev - in', ba - by;
it __ seems to fall a - part, __ keep on be - liev - in', ba - by;

just be true __ to your heart.
just be true __ to your heart.

Repeat and Fade

Optional Ending

TRULY, MADLY, DEEPLY

Words and Music by DANIEL JONE
and DARREN HAYE

I'll be your dream, I'll be your wish, I'll be your fan-ta-sy. I'll be your hope, I'll be your love, Be ev-ery-thing that you need. __ I'll love you more with ev-ery breath, Tru-ly, mad-ly, deep-ly do. __ I will be strong, I will be faith-ful 'cause I'm count-ing on a new be-gin-ning. A

WATERFALLS

Words and Music by MARQUEZE ETHERIDG
LISA NICOLE LOPES, RICO R. WAD
PAT BROWN and RAMON MURRA

Relaxed R&B shuffle

A lone-ly moth-er gaz-ing out of her win-dow star-ing
Lit-tle pre-cious has a nat-'ral ob-ses — sion for temp

Eb   Bb(add9)

gon - na have it your way or noth - ing at all, but I think you're

Dbmaj7   Ab(add9)

Repeat and Fade

mov - ing too fast. __

Additional Lyrics

Rap: **I seen a rainbow yesterday**
But too many storms have come and gone
Leavin' a trace of not one God-given ray
Is it because my life is ten shades of gray
I pray all ten fade away
Seldom praise Him for the sunny days
And like His promise is true
Only my faith can undo
The many chances I blew
To bring my life to anew
Clear blue and unconditional skies
Have dried the tears from my eyes
No more lonely cries
My only bleedin' hope
Is for the folk who can't cope
Wit such an endurin' pain
That it keeps 'em in the pourin' rain
Who's to blame
For tootin' caine in your own vein
What a shame
You shoot and aim for someone else's brain
You claim the insane
And name this day in time
For fallin' prey to crime
I say the system got you victim to your own mind
Dreams are hopeless aspirations
In hopes of comin' true
Believe in yourself
The rest is up to me and you

WHEN THE LIGHTS GO OUT

Words and Music by ELIOT KENNEDY,
SEAN CONLON, JASON BROWN, RICHARD DOBSON,
RICHARD BREEN, SCOTT ROBINSON, TIM LEVER,
MIKE PERCY and JOHN McCLAUGHLIN

me when the lights ___ go out. *(Rap:) It's a blackout girl, the lights are off. I can*

feel you gettin' closer, now take your clothes off. *Your body looks so soft.* *In between the sheets*

I lay you down, girl. I wanna knock your socks off, *knock your block off. Girl, I'm down for whatever.*

There are few things that's forever, like you in my life, girl, that's all that I need to get by.

Time to break it down 'cause you're makin' me high.

Ba - by, when the lights go out ev - 'ry sin - gle word could not ex -

press the love and ten - der - ness. I'll show you what it's all a - bout. Babe,__ I swear you will suc - cumb to

Repeat and Fade

Optional Ending

me. So, ba - by, come to me. Ba - by, when the me.

WIDE OPEN SPACES

Words and Music by
SUSAN GIBSON

Who does-n't know what I'm talk-ing a-bout?